MAPS AND SYMBOLS

ANGELA ROYSTON

WAYLAND

GEOGRAPHY STARTS HERE!
Maps and Symbols

OTHER TITLES IN THE SERIES
Hills and Mountains · Rivers and Streams
Weather Around You · Where People Live
Your Environment

Produced for Wayland Publishers Limited by

Lionheart Books

10, Chelmsford Square

London NW10 3AR

England

Designer: Ben White

Editor: Lionel Bender

Picture Research: Madeleine Samuel

Electronic make-up: Mike Pilley, Radius

Illustrated by Rudi Visi

First Published in 1998 by Wayland Publishers Limited

61 Western Road, Hove, East Sussex BN3 1JD

© **Copyright 1998 Wayland Publishers Limited**

Find Wayland on the Internet at http://www.wayland.co.uk

British Library Cataloguing in Publication Data

Vaughan, Jenny,

Maps and symbols. – (Geography starts here!)

1. Maps– Juvenile literature 2. Map reading – Juvenile literature

I. Title II. Bender, Lionel

912

ISBN 0 7502 1987 4

Printed and bound by Eurografica, Vicenza, Italy

Picture Acknowledgements

Page 1: Eye Ubiquitous/Paul Seheult. 5 Getty Images. 6: Zefa Photo Library/Stockmarket. 8: Wayland Picture Library. 11: Eye Ubiquitous/Gavin Wickham. 12: Zefa Photo Library. 15: Ecoscene/Hulme. 16: Eye Ubiquitous/Steve Brock. 19: James Davis Photography. 21: Neil Jinkerson/Tim Hunt of Jarrold Publishing. 23: Zefa/Streichan. 24: Eye Ubiquitous/B. Spencer. 25: Zefa Photo Library. 26: Aerofilms Limited. 28, 29: Wayland Picture Library. Cover Photo: Zefa Photo Library.

The photo on page 1 shows schoolchildren using maps and compasses to find directions.

CONTENTS

Chapter 1 WHAT IS A MAP? 4–5

Chapter 2 WHERE ARE YOU? 6–13
Bird's-Eye View 8
Which Way? 10
North, East, South and West 12

Chapter 3 MAPS AND GRIDS 14–19
Mapping the Land 16
Maps of the World 18

Chapter 4 SCALE 20–23
Contours 22

Chapter 5 SYMBOLS 24–27
Colours and Shapes 26

Chapter 6 DRAWING A MAP 28–29
Map Facts and Figures 30
Further Reading 30
Glossary 31
Index 32

WHAT IS A MAP?

A map is a drawing that shows the shape of a place and the things that are there. Some maps can show a small place, such as a room. Other maps can show the whole world.

If you know how to read a map, it shows you where places are and helps you find your way.

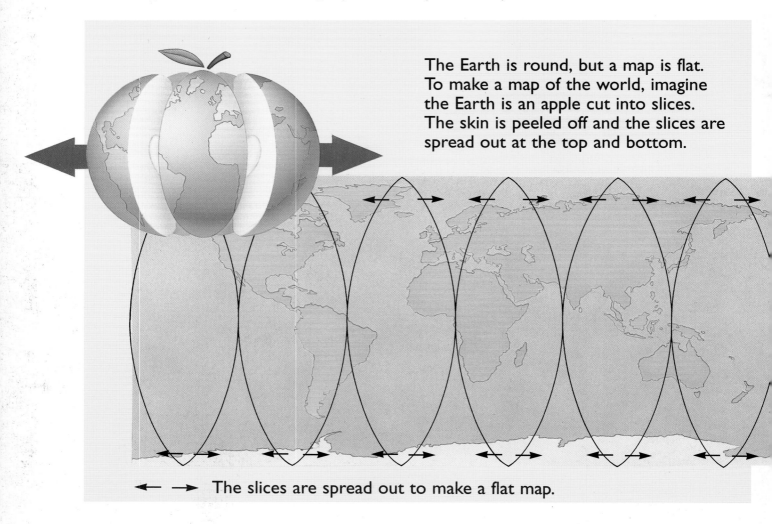

The Earth is round, but a map is flat. To make a map of the world, imagine the Earth is an apple cut into slices. The skin is peeled off and the slices are spread out at the top and bottom.

← → The slices are spread out to make a flat map.

Satellites take photos of
the Earth from space.
The photos are then
used to make accurate
maps of the world.

WHERE ARE YOU?

Some words tell you where something or someone is. In a game of hide-and-seek, you might look for people under the beds, behind the chairs or inside the wardrobes.

A flying bird sees the ground from above. This 'bird's-eye view' shows roads going under and over one another.

In hide-and-seek, the words 'under', 'behind' and 'inside' describe where the people could be compared to things you can see. Maps show where things are compared to each other.

In this bird's-eye-view of an imaginary town, see how the words 'above', 'on top of', 'in front of' or 'next to', describe where things are.

The satellite dishes are on top of the buildings.

The car is in front of the houses.

The birds are above the buildings.

The lorry is next to the hedge.

7

A Bird's-Eye View

The best way to see exactly where things are is to look down on them from above. A picture or drawing that shows a place from above is called a bird's-eye view or a plan.

A plan of a room shows the floor space that items take up. A map is a bird's eye view of a place with symbols to show what things are.

Things that you are used to seeing from the side can often look strange from above.

DRAW A PLAN

Imagine that you are a fly on the ceiling of your bedroom. Draw a plan view of your room. Remember to show just the top of your bed, chest of drawers, and so on. Do not try to show the sides or the height of things.

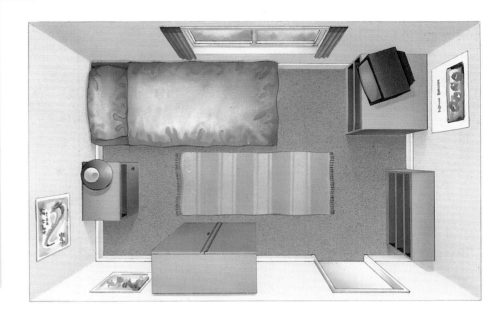

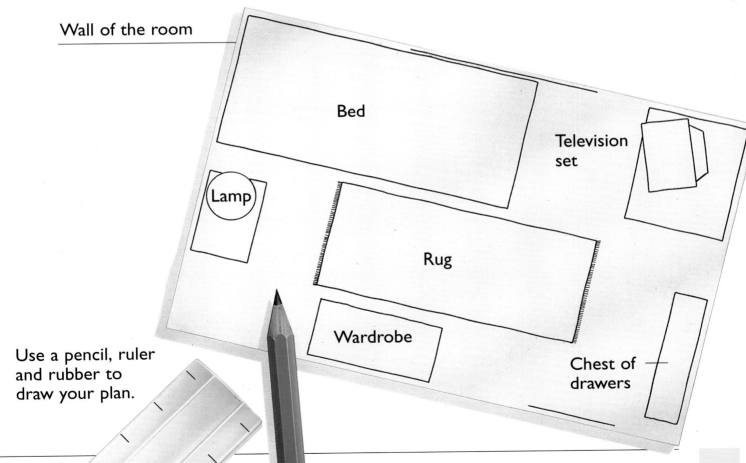

Wall of the room

Bed

Television set

Lamp

Rug

Wardrobe

Chest of drawers

Use a pencil, ruler and rubber to draw your plan.

9

Which Way?

If you told a visitor the way to your school, you would probably use the phrases 'turn left', 'turn right' and 'go straight on'.

The words 'left' and 'right' tell you on which side something is. When you go straight ahead, you are moving forwards.

FIND YOUR WAY

Use the words 'left', 'right' and 'straight on' to describe how to get to the school from the house on this map. Follow the arrows to help you find your way.

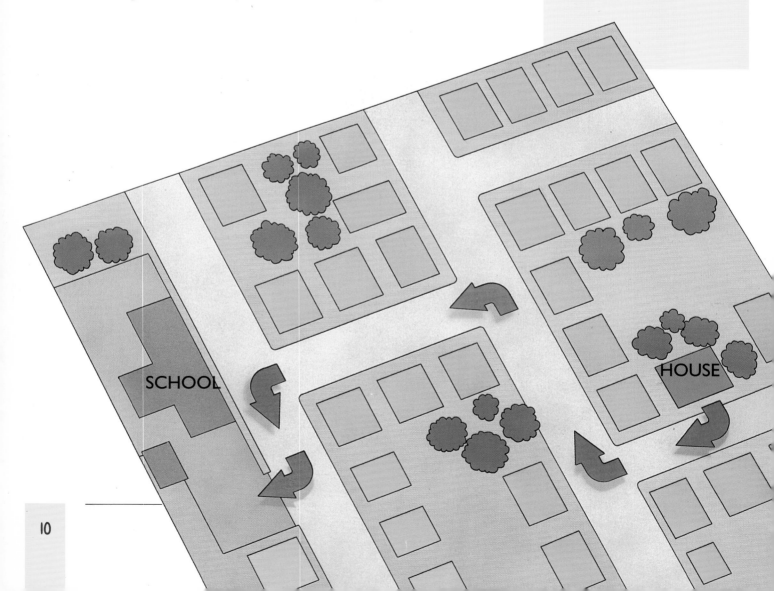

With the words forwards, backwards, left and right, you can give directions to anywhere in your neighbourhood. A map puts directions into a drawing.

In this bird's-eye view of a town, what directions would you give a driver to go from A to B? (Answer on page 32.)

The cockerel on this weather vane turns to show the direction the wind is coming from.

North, East, South and West

For long distances, people give directions using the words north, south, east and west.

Maps are usually drawn with north at the top and south at the bottom. East is then to the right and west to the left.

USE A COMPASS

A compass is used to find directions on a map. Place the compass on top of your map. Keep the compass and map flat. Line up the map so that the north point of the compass needle lines up with north on the map.

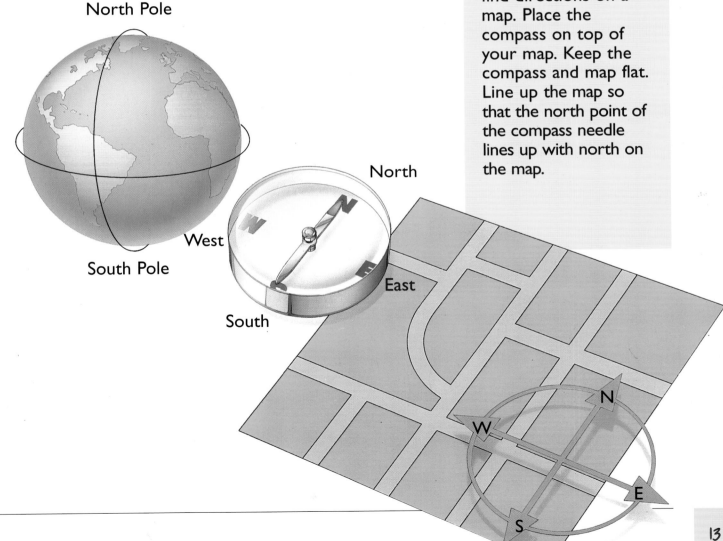

North Pole

South Pole

North

West

East

South

N

W

E

S

MAPS AND GRIDS

Maps are usually drawn on squared paper. The pattern of lines across and down the paper is called a grid. The sides of the squares are given numbers or letters.

Things can be found on a map by saying the letter and number of the square in which it sits. Large items may fill several squares.

These scientists are using a grid to record which type of plant grows where.

Suppose you are told that the place you want is in C8. Instead of looking on the whole map, you just have to look in that square.

Placing a grid over the map below makes it much easier to find a particular landmark.

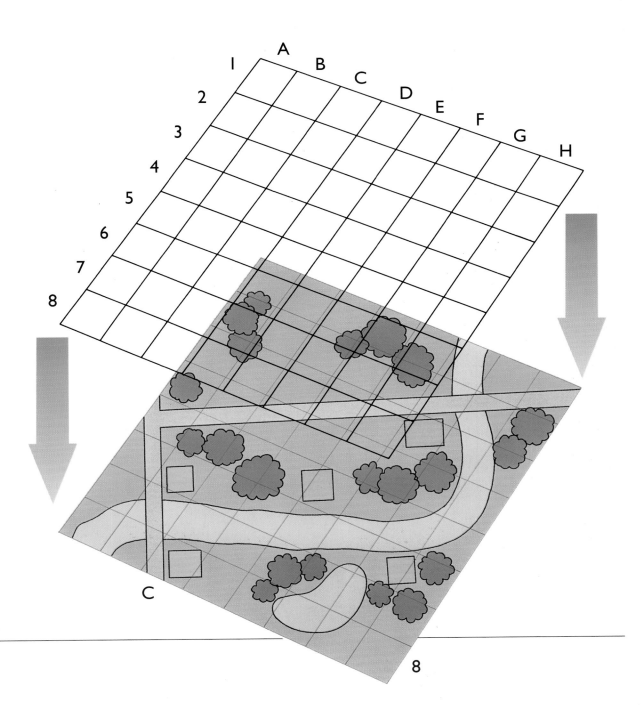

Mapping the Land

Maps of the countryside have a grid. Map-makers use special instruments to find which places are on a straight line.

Aeroplanes and satellites take bird's-eye-view photographs to help the map-makers draw their maps.

A surveyor uses a telescope-like instrument to measure distances and plot a straight line across the countryside.

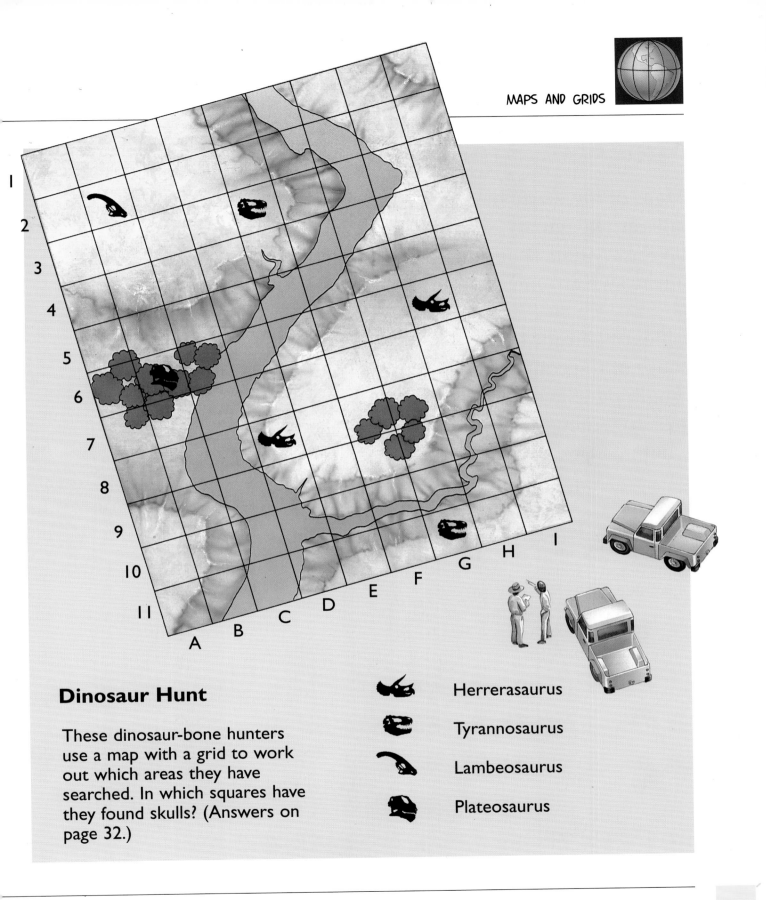

Dinosaur Hunt

These dinosaur-bone hunters use a map with a grid to work out which areas they have searched. In which squares have they found skulls? (Answers on page 32.)

Herrerasaurus

Tyrannosaurus

Lambeosaurus

Plateosaurus

Maps of the World

Maps of the world have grids, too. The grid lines are imaginary, so you will not see them on the ground. The equator is an imaginary line drawn around the middle of the world.

Lines of latitude tell you how far north or south of the equator you are. Lines of longitude tell you how far east or west you are. Together, these lines tell you exactly where you are on a map.

A globe is a ball, or sphere, on which is drawn a map of the Earth.

North Pole

Greenwich Meridian – the first and last line of latitude.

Equator – the central line of longitude.

At sea, there are no signs to guide you. Sailors use special instruments to find out where they are.

SCALE

A map can show a large area, such as a whole country, or a smaller area, for example part of a country or just a town or city. The scale on a map tells you how much smaller the map is compared to the real thing.

When you know the scale, you can work out distances on the ground from distances on the map.

This series of maps shows the scale getting bigger from the map on the left to the one on the right.

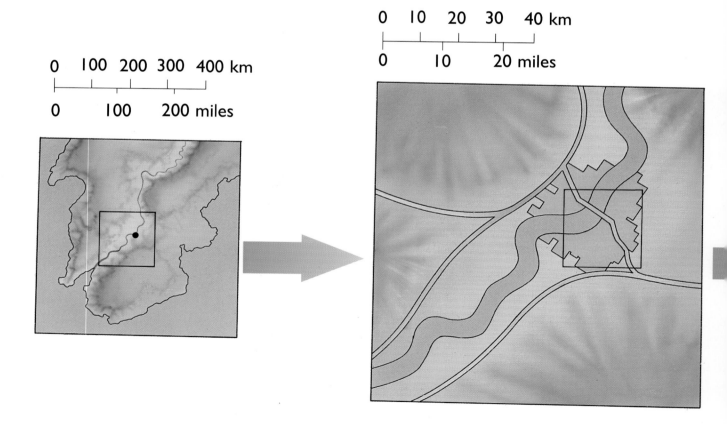

In this model village, the buildings are 20 times smaller than the real ones. The scale of the models is written as 1/20th, or 1:20.

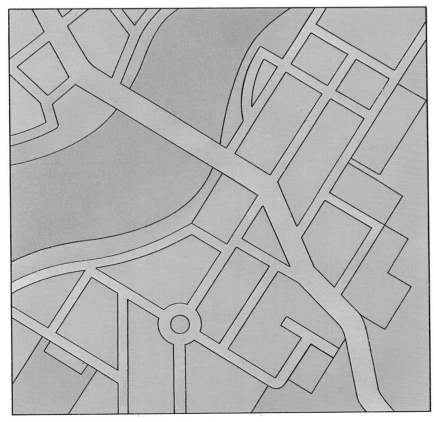

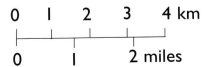

0   1   2   3   4 km

0   1   2 miles

Contours

Maps are flat, but the land has mountains, hills and valleys. Map-makers cannot show height on a flat piece of paper. Instead, they use different colours and contour lines to show how high different places are.

The contour lines on a map each have a number or measurement. This measurement tells you the height of that line above sea level.

Contour lines show the shape of high ground as though it went up in steps. Each contour line joins up places that are the same height.

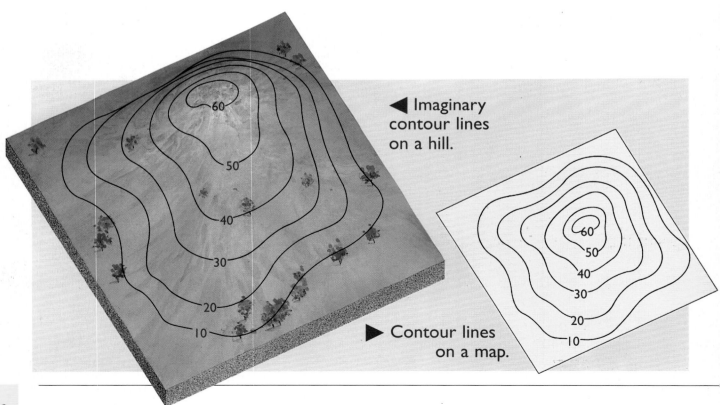

◄ Imaginary contour lines on a hill.

► Contour lines on a map.

These hills slope down into a valley. When a hill slopes steeply, the contour lines on the map are close together.

SYMBOLS

A map can never show you everything. Map-makers have to choose the most important things to show. They use symbols to fit in more information and to make maps easier and quicker to read.

Rivers, lakes, roads and towns all have special symbols. Some symbols use colour. Others are a special shape.

This traveller is looking at a map of Paris to find her way round the city. The symbols show important landmarks.

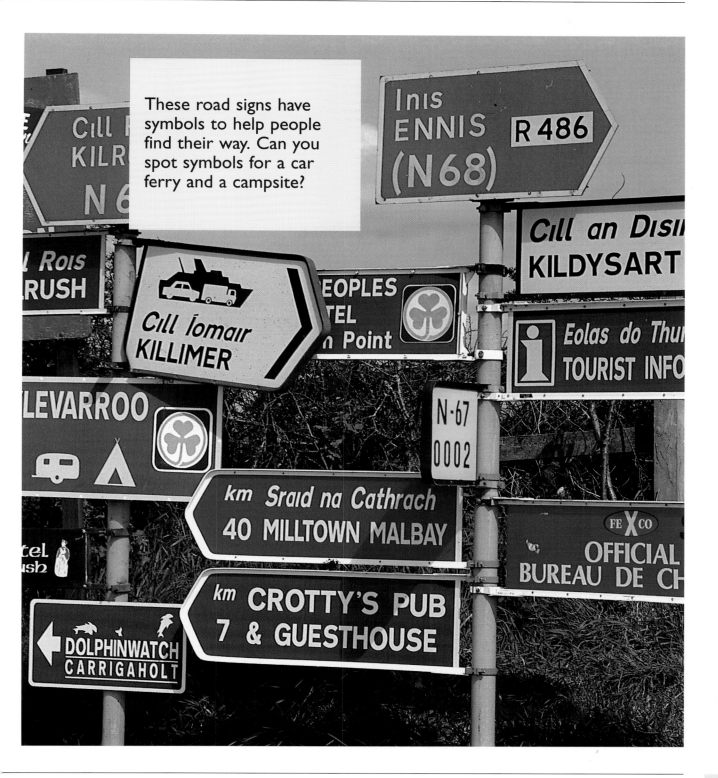

These road signs have symbols to help people find their way. Can you spot symbols for a car ferry and a campsite?

Colours and Shapes

Symbols are only useful if everyone can understand them. A map key, or legend, shows what each symbol means.

Maps the world over do not all use the same symbol for each thing. Mountains may be shown by colour or by pyramid-like shapes. Roads may be coloured red, green or yellow.

On a map of the area shown below, the roads, river, fields and houses would each be shown by a different symbol.

MAP SYMBOLS

Why not design your own map symbols for landmarks or types of road around where you live? Remember, symbols need to be easy to understand. Think about what you want to show and then think about the best colour and shape to use.

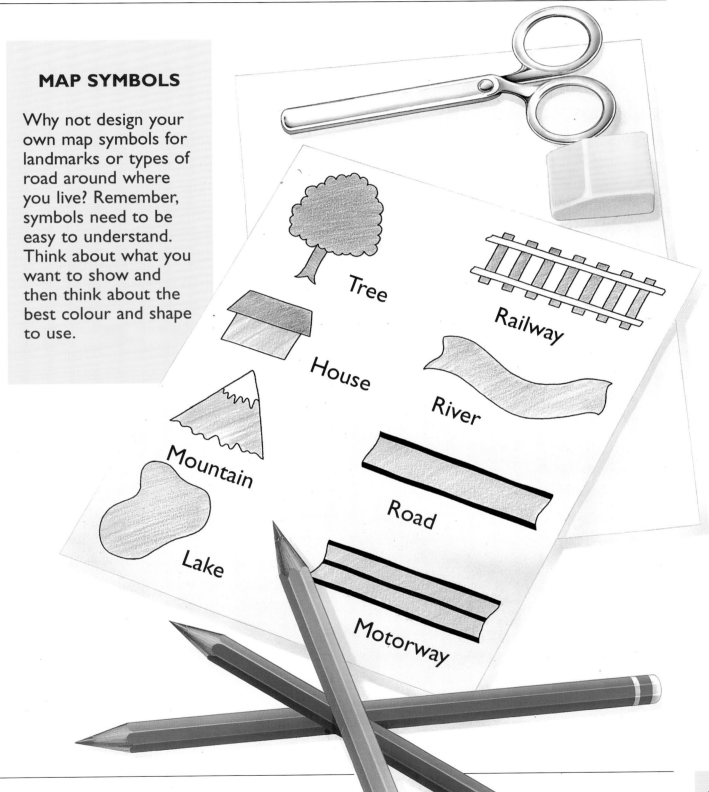

Tree

House

Mountain

Lake

Railway

River

Road

Motorway

27

DRAWING A MAP

Before making a map, you have to decide what kind of map it is going to be. Some maps show countries and cities. Others show weather or tourist sites.

Symbols on a map show important landmarks, such as roads, hills, rivers, railway tracks and houses or towns. Colours show water, forests, low ground and high ground.

This girl is making a weather map. She places symbols for clouds, rain and the Sun on a map to show what the weather will be like.

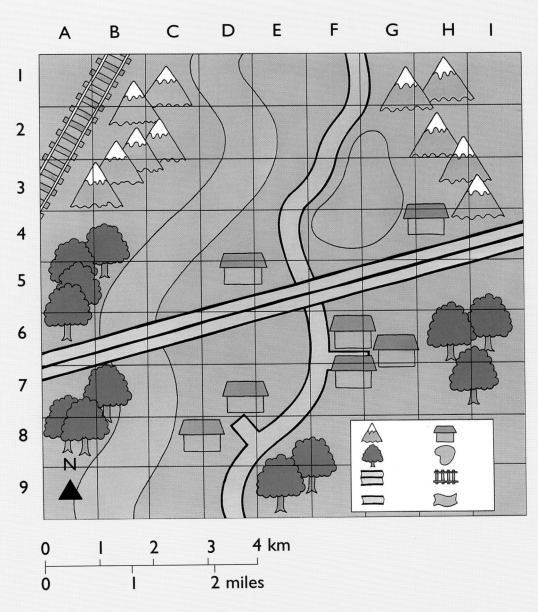

Find a map of your neighbourhood. Draw a simple grid on tracing paper. Lay your grid over the map and carefully trace your journey home from school. Add some symbols to your map for landmarks that you pass on your journey. Colour in your map and give it a key.

MAP FACTS AND FIGURES

Earth measurements
The equator is 40,075 kilometres long. The distance between the North and South Poles is 20,003 kilometres.

North Pole
There are really two North Poles. The geographic North Pole is where all lines of longitude meet. Compass needles, however, point to the magnetic North Pole, about 1,600 kilometres away.

First to reach the North Pole
On 6 April 1909, the Arctic explorers Robert Peary and Matthew Henson reached the North Pole. Frederick Cook claimed that he had reached the Pole first, in 1908, but his claim was never proved.

South Pole
The South Pole is in Antarctica and is 2,800 metres above sea level.

First to reach the South Pole
In 1911 Norwegian explorer Roald Amundsen and British explorer Robert Scott each led a team towards the South Pole. Amundsen won the race on 14 December. Scott and his team reached the South Pole a month later, but died on the journey back.

First compass
The Ancient Chinese were the first to use a magnetic compass. They used lodestone, a stone containing iron which is naturally magnetic. In the 1100s, sailors in the Mediterranean used lodestone compasses to help them find their way.

Computerized compass
GPS (Global Positioning System) uses radio signals beamed from a satellite circling the Earth and a computer to tell you where you are, wherever you are.

Pole Star
On a clear night, the Pole Star shows the direction of north if you are north of the equator. The Southern Cross points to the south if you are south of the equator.

Oldest map
The oldest known map is over 5,000 years old and was made in Sumeria. It was drawn on to a clay block and shows the plan of an estate.

First geography book
The Earth was shown as a round flat circle in a book produced by the Ancient Greeks 2,600 years ago.

East or west?
In 1492 Christopher Columbus sailed west from Spain expecting to find a new route to China and India in the east. When he reached the Caribbean islands he thought they were part of Asia and called them the West Indies.

Further Reading

Investigating Maps by Susan Montford (Young Library Limited, 1993).

Maps and Globes by Sabrina Crew (Watts, 1996).

Maps and Mazes: A First Guide to Map Making by Gillian Chapman (Macdonald Young Books, 1993).

Maps and Mapping by Barbara Taylor (Kingfisher, 1994).

Mapwork 1 by David Flint and Mandy Suhr (Wayland, 1992). Also available as a *Big Book of Mapwork 1* (Wayland, 1998). Worksheets to accompany Mapwork 1 will be available in mid-1998).

Mapwork 2 by David Flint and Mandy Suhr (Wayland, 1992).

Philip's Picture Atlas for Children (Heinemann, 1995).

GLOSSARY

Compass An instrument for finding directions. A compass needle is magnetic and always points to magnetic north.

Contour A line on a map that joins places which are the same height above sea level.

Equator An imaginary line on a map drawn around the middle of the Earth.

Key A list of the symbols used on a map with their meanings.

Latitude Lines Lines drawn on a map from east to west. They show how far north or south a place is compared to the equator. The equator is the line of latitude 0 degrees.

Longitude Lines Lines drawn on a map from the North Pole to the South Pole. The Greenwich Meridian runs through London and is the line of longitude 0 degrees. Other lines of longitude show how far east or west a place is compared to the Greenwich Meridian.

Scale A way of showing large distances on the ground by short distances on a map or plan.

Sea level The surface of the sea.

Symbol A shape or drawing that represents something.

Schoolchildren study a globe to find the latitude and longitude of their city.

INDEX

bird's-eye view 6, 7, 8, 11, 16

colours, use of 22, 26, 28
compass 13, 30, 31
contour lines 22, 23, 31

directions 11, 12, 13
distance 16, 20

Earth 4, 5
east 13, 18
equator 18, 30, 31

Global Positioning Sysytem 30
globe 18
Greenwich Meridian 18

grid 14–18

height of land 22
key 26–31

latitude 18, 31
legend 26
longitude 18, 30, 31

maps 4, 6, 13, 14, 16, 18, 20, 21, 28, 29
  making 16, 22, 26, 28
  of the world 4, 5, 18
  reading 4

north 13, 18
North Pole 30

plan (of a room) 8, 9
Pole Star 30

scale 20–21, 31
sea level 22, 31
shapes, use of 26
south 13, 18
South Pole 30
surveyors 16
symbols 8, 24–28, 31

weather map 28
weather vane 12
west 13, 18

Answers to questions in this book:

Page 11: To get from A to B on the photograph, the driver needs to go straight to the end of the road, turn left, then take the first turning on the right and follow the road round.

Page 17: Skulls were found in squares B2, B6, D8, E3, G11 and H6.